God is answering your every command that you affirm to be true for yourself and your life! Once you think of new thoughts about all that you truly want, you must feel it to be already yours and then be grateful that it is yours! It is done! It is yours to come!

You must genuinely believe in it and then it comes into your life. It is so very magical, the way that it works! This is when you gain your amazing power to receive all of your desires and abundance for your life!

You are living on this glorious amazing planet and you are given this amazing power within your mind to achieve anything that you truly want. There are no limits to what you can create in life and you must realize all of the magic that you have within yourself! Your mind is so powerful and magnificently amazing! It is so crazy wonderfully magical!

Once you live your life filled with amazing purpose, helping others to succeed daily and hold gratitude for this amazing beautiful life. Everything in your life will change for the better and abundance will flow into your life!

To make a positive difference in the lives around you each day for the greater good! I can't think of anything more important than learning while helping others and living all of your amazing dreams in life!

The internet has completely changed the entire world and it is always changing more with time. No returning to the old ways of only working for money and not knowing the information that we need to achieve things.

Everything is right at our fingertips and we can pretty much learn anything now and we can become anything that we want to be! All we need to do is search it on the internet and study and apply what we have learned!

Your mind is so powerful, everything that you dream about, all of your thoughts, and feelings daily. This is exactly what you will attract into your life and all of the people that will help you to achieve it all. All of the abundance and success that you crave can be truly yours, once you gain awareness and gratitude!

So if you want to make changes within your life, it all starts with you shifting your mindset and attitude daily to make a huge difference in the world and the people around you!

You most definitely have the power, to shift your mind daily to attract anything that you want into your life and it is that simple! It all starts with you! To bless everything in the world and to wish the very best for everyone!

To live with a humble heart, to overcome the adversity in your life, and to push forward to achieve the amazing dreams that you hold within your magnificent mind!

To help, to support others daily while becoming a better person by making positive changes daily in the world! This is the recipe for success in life and it all starts by giving more and helping more people daily!

Once you realize that your power comes from your daily awareness of everything around you. You then start to see magic everywhere, with abundance and opportunities!

Every possibility already exists within you, all inventions to be created and they are waiting for your human mind to expand and to believe it!

Everything in the universe is connected and it is up to us to realize this power to achieve our dreams! We must feel the energy from our mind and we must focus on the good and the goodness within our mind. It all comes from our amazing mindset to push through the hard times to create the life of our amazing beautiful dreams!

My book will completely change your life for the better! It will help you to realize your true self-worth, and this all comes by increasing your value about things within your life. It will help you to find your true amazing purpose and to awaken your awareness of the things around you!

You will start to have an abundance mentality and attitude of gratitude for this amazing life. Such a burning desire to help others to succeed daily and to focus on your amazing dreams!

RAINBOW FOCUS

Every day we are all creating things, trying to make a better future for ourselves and to leave a legacy behind! With our amazing thoughts, wisdom, and understanding, we can all achieve incredible greatness!

When you build your life from your wisdom, understanding, and your ability to help others to succeed each day! You will be much happier, more energized and you will make a huge difference in the lives of the people around you!

Your self-growth will be so very incredible, as you read through the Affirmations in my book." Each one of her quotes are magical, when used daily in your life, they will create happiness and abundance for you.

As an international Best-Selling Author, I will show you my great strength about how I went through adversity, heartache, and pain. How I pushed through it all, by not giving up on my dreams and by changing my daily mindset! Now I am an amazingly successful entrepreneur, achieving my amazing beautiful dreams.

So once you realize that you can achieve anything, once you start to change your mindset and focus daily on everything that you want to create! Abundance will flow into your life and you will see yourself living the amazing beautiful life that you always wanted for yourself! It all starts with you!

As you travel through the magnificent pages of this amazing book, you will learn some amazing techniques and ways to change your life around! You will come to know how you can be happy, and achieve almost anything that you want in life. You will discover who you truly are and all of the magic happiness and incredible abundance that is waiting for your life!

CHERYL ZHANG INTERNATIONAL BEST-SELLING AUTHOR, SPEAKER & MOTIVATIONAL LIFE COACH.

RAINBOW FOCUS

RAINBOW FOCUS AFFIRMATIONS

By: Cheryl Zhang

Inspiration #1

Fear or Trust?

They both are invisible.

One leads to freedom. Which one do you think it is?

Affirmation

♥ I have the power to choose trust over fear

♥ My time is coming, I can see a beautiful rainbow.

Inspiration #2

Have the trust and courage to move through your fears.

You'll find freedom on the other side.

Affirmation

♥ I have the courage to face my fears

♥ I believe I can overcome all of my fears

Inspiration #3

Trust creates abundant inner peace.

Inner peace is the path to creating abundance
in your physical world.

Affirmation

♥ I believe in my ability to create peace in my
life

♥ I trust that peace leads to abundance for me

Inspiration #4

Gratitude is a part of trust. Some people think "I will be grateful when abundance comes."

Abundance will only come to you when you find gratitude now.

Affirmation

♥ I am grateful for all parts of my life

RAINBOW FOCUS

Inspiration #5

Thank you for working all things together for something greater in my life.

Even grief and loss.

Affirmation

♥ Grief and loss are preparation for something greater

Inspiration #6

If massive good didn't come from grief and loss, it wouldn't be allowed.

Start looking for the good in these experiences.

Affirmation

♥ I choose to see the good in grief and loss

Inspiration #7

Beauty and freedom will always come from the ashes.

Look closely so you don't miss them!

Affirmation

♥ I believe grief and loss can produce freedom & happiness

Inspiration #8

Finding gratitude for grief and loss will help you move past it faster than anything else.

I know it's hard to do.

When you do it, freedom follows for you.

Affirmation

♥ I am grateful for the grief and loss I have experienced in my life

♥ Grief and loss have prepared me for something bigger

RAINBOW FOCUS

♥ My time is coming for me

Inspiration #9

Never give up. Never settle.

Keep trying until you find what you deserve.

It will come at the right time.

Affirmation

♥ I promise to never give up on myself

♥ I promise to never settle for less than i
deserve

Inspiration #10

Let's make sure to release any limiting beliefs
that could be holding us back from the best.

RAINBOW FOCUS

Let yourself believe you deserve the best,

instead of feeling unworthy.

Affirmation

♥ I deserve the best that life has to offer

♥ All things are possible when you believe

Inspiration #11

Thank you for bringing me the best.

Thank you for helping me grow, so I'm ready
to receive the best.

Affirmation

♥ I want to become the best so I know I'm
ready to receive the best.

♥ I am becoming the best version of myself

♥ I open myself to receive the best

Inspiration #12

Thank you for blessing me with deeply
fulfilling pleasures of all kinds.

May they brighten my light and my days.

Affirmation

♥ I open myself to receive truly fulfilling pleasures

RAINBOW FOCUS

Inspiration #13

Today I wish you the fulfilling pleasure of simplicity.

May it bring you peace and comfort.

Affirmation

♥ I want more simplicity in my life

♥ I receive simplicity

Inspiration #14

To create more of the fulfilling pleasure of simplicity, find a singular thought and focus on it.

Make sure it's a positive one.

Affirmation

♥ I have the power to focus on a single thought

Inspiration #14

A singular positive thought will bring peace to
a complicated mind.

It will calm the "what if's" and the doubts.

It will push aside fear and keep you in
alignment.

Affirmation

♥ I receive the peace and calm a single
thought brings

RAINBOW FOCUS

Inspiration #15

The next step is to trust that your deepest
desire will happen.

Create a statement that reflects this belief.

Focus on this belief until it becomes reality.

Affirmation

♥ I trust my deepest desire will happen at the right time

Inspiration #16

I receive all types of divine happiness.

I receive them without trying to control what they look like or how they arrive.

Affirmation

♥ I am open to receive divine happiness & abundance in my life

Inspiration #17

Divine happiness is available to those who believe all things are possible.

Affirmation

♥ I believe all things are possible with God.

Inspiration #18

Those who are truly happy, free their soul and follow its guidance.

Affirmation

RAINBOW FOCUS

♥ I want to free my soul

♥ I want to follow my souls guidance & help
myself & others succced

Inspiration #19

When you follow your soul things can become uncomfortable for a time.

Keep going and trust the process. The freedom is so worth it.

Affirmation

♥ When things are uncomfortable I choose to trust the process

♥ My time is coming

Inspiration #20

We should all strive to love each other with
unconditional love.

Sometimes that means setting boundaries that
are healthy for both of you.

This can equal freedom for both of you if
done with love.

Affirmation

♥ I want to love without conditions

♥ I want to experience the life changing
power of loving boundaries

Inspiration #21

RAINBOW FOCUS

Let's love others unconditionally so they can put down their burden of perfection.

Perfection can't live where love resides.

Affirmation

♥ I will use love to free others from perfection

♥ I will use love to free myself from perfection

Inspiration #22

Don't forget to love yourself unconditionally.
You deserve love no matter what.

Give yourself permission to make choices that
are good for you and your future.

Affirmation

♥ I want to love myself unconditionally

♥ I am working on loving myself

♥ I do love myself & others too

(choose whichever one feels aligned or right for you)

Inspiration #23

Learning to love unconditionally will enable life to love you in return.

RAINBOW FOCUS

What you put out there is what comes back to you, what you give is what you will get in return

Affirmation

♥ I believe if I give love it will come back to me in unexpected ways

Inspiration #24

The dream you've had for such a long time.
The one you're tempted to give up on.

Don't. Sometimes it can take many decades to
come true. The trick is to keep pressing

forward no matter what.

Affirmation

♥ I vow to keep moving toward my dream no matter what happens in my life and i will love everyone always.

Inspiration #25

When your dream becomes a reality, you'll be so grateful you didn't give up. You will deeply appreciate it and never take it for granted.

Affirmation

♥ When my dream comes true, I vow never

take it for granted

Inspiration #26

When fighting for your dream to come true, gratitude is helpful. Say to the divine or the future, "Thank you for bringing stability and abundance to my life".

Affirmation

♥ I will make an effort to grateful every day

♥ I trust that gratitude will help my dream become a reality

Inspiration #27

It's time to believe you are worthy of your
dream. You are worthy of love. You are
worthy of stability and abundance. You are
worthy of health and vitality. You are worthy
of happiness.

46

RAINBOW FOCUS

Affirmation

♥ I want to believe I am worthy of my dream

♥ I will grow into the person who is ready to receive my dream

♥ I am worthy of my dream

(choose whichever one feels aligned or right for you)

Inspiration #28

On your way to finding a dream come true
you will encounter many twists and turns.

Trust the process.

Affirmation

♥ It's okay to trust the process that God has
for me

♥ I want to trust the process for my life

♥ I am trusting the process of my life

♥ I trust the process of my life

RAINBOW FOCUS

(choose whichever one feels aligned or right

for you)

Inspiration #29

One day all those twists and turns will make

sense.

They are working for you not against you.
They are preparing you for something greater.

RAINBOW FOCUS

Affirmation

♥ One day it will all make perfect sense

♥ Twists and turns are preparing me for
something greater

Inspiration #30

Even if everything looks like it's falling apart, keep believing.

Everything is working on your behalf to help your dreams come true.

Affirmation

♥ Everything is working on my behalf and for my best interest

Inspiration #31

Some of our darkest moments carry with them the brightest blessings.

Look for the good in them. I guarantee good is there if you look hard enough.

Affirmation

RAINBOW FOCUS

♥ Help me find the good in dark and difficult times

♥ I trust I will find the good

♥ Blessings are coming my way

Inspiration #32

On your journey to your dreams, it is necessary to find certainty. Certainty will give you patience and persistence required. Certainty comes from within.

Affirmation

♥ Certainty will give me patience and persistence

♥ I desire greater certainty

RAINBOW FOCUS

Inspiration #33

Certainty about your dreams will help you
close and open the right doors. Choose wisely!
Your soul (intuition/gut) knows the way.

Affirmation

♥ Certainty closes and opens doors for me

♥ I will listen to my soul/inner knowing to help me choose the right path that God wants for my life

Inspiration #34

When you are certain it creates stability. We all crave stability.

Stability is at the core of all our dreams.

Affirmation

♥ Certainty creates stability

♥ I believe I deserve stability

♥ Stability is on its way to me

Inspiration #35

On the road to your dreams, trust that everything that happens is guiding you to stability. Even when things feel unstable.

Affirmation

♥ I trust that everything is guiding me to stability

♥ My time is coming for happiness & abundance

RAINBOW FOCUS

Inspiration #36

Finding things to look forward to will keep
you joyful. Even in the darkest of times.

RAINBOW FOCUS

This is a must as you work toward your
dreams.

Affirmation

♥ I am looking forward to abundance

♥ I am excited for my life and dreams to
come true for me

Inspiration #37

Your trials will not leave you empty handed.

Look for the blessings coming from them.
Sometimes we have to look a little harder, but
they are there.

Affirmation

♥ Blessings come from each trial

♥ I see lots of blessings coming to me

Inspiration #38

On the path to your dreams, do what lights
you up and motivates you.

That's your soul guiding you. It knows the
way.

Affirmation

♥ I am doing something that lights me up
each day

Inspiration #39

Be persistent and consistent as you work
toward your dreams. Persistence and
consistency keep the much needed
momentum going. If you only have the
strength to do one thing, do that one thing.
And do it well.

Affirmation

♥ I will be persistent and consistent

RAINBOW FOCUS

♥ I am working on becoming persistent and consistent

♥ I am consistent and persistent & determined to succeed

(choose whichever one feels aligned or right for you)

Inspiration #40

65

When we are working toward our dreams it's important to remember one thing.

We are mining for gold. Diamonds are much harder to find, but so worth the extra effort. Don't settle for anything less. And don't be that guy who quit just before striking gold but be the one who keeps pushing towards finding the beautiful diamonds

Affirmation

♥ I will not settle

♥ I will keep going until my soul is satisfied

Inspiration #41

We must believe the right people will arrive at the right time. We are not supposed to do everything alone. We do need help on occasion. Find people you can trust to help guide you to where you want to go.

Affirmation

♥ The right people will arrive at the right time

Inspiration #42

RAINBOW FOCUS

When clarity comes, relief is right behind it.
Look forward to clarity so you can look
forward to relief.

Affirmation

♥ Thank you for bringing me clarity

♥ Thank you for bringing me relief

RAINBOW FOCUS

Inspiration #43

When relief comes, embrace the peace and joy
that comes with it. Let these energies take you
where you need to go.

Affirmation

♥ Thank you for relief

♥ Thank you for bringing me peace

♥ Thank you for bringing me joy

Inspiration #44

It's important to trust the journey. All the twists and turns are leading to something good.

Affirmation

♥ I chose to trust the journey God has for me

♥ I chose to trust the twists and turns

Inspiration #45

Everything is going to work out somehow. A way will be made where you cannot see one. The best is yet to come.

Affirmation

♥ It'll all workout

♥ Thank you for making a way where I cannot see one

♥ The best is coming

Inspiration #46

Let things work in your favor. I know it's hard to do sometimes. But it's well worth it in the end.

Affirmation

RAINBOW FOCUS

♥ Help me let go so things can work in my favor

♥ Please keep me from sabotaging what's coming

Inspiration #47

It's time to look forward to the good things to come. Even if you can't see them or know what they are.

Affirmation

♥ Thank you for the good that's coming

♥ Help me trust it's there even though I can't see it

♥ What's happening is preparing me to take me higher

Inspiration #48

Just think, today could be the day that things
go right. The unknown comes with unseen
good stuff and possibilities of breakthroughs.

77

Affirmation

♥ Today could be the day things go right

Inspiration #49

RAINBOW FOCUS

Look forward to today's surprises. You never know where they come from or what they look like. But each day has good surprises for you.

Affirmation

♥ Thank you for good surprises today

♥ Thank you for good surprises tomorrow

Inspiration #50

When good ideas come to you, follow them.
Take action on them. One can never tell
where it might lead.

Affirmation

♥ I trust in the good ideas that come to me

♥ I am looking forward to seeing where they

take me

Inspiration #51

RAINBOW FOCUS

Today I wish for you fun surprises and beautiful blessings. With them will come smiles and joy and hope. Hope that says you matter.

Affirmation

♥ Smiles, joy and renewed hope are coming my way

♥ I matter in this world

♥ My time is coming

Inspiration #52

It's amazing what happens when we are loved
the right way. It changes our lives almost
instantly. It strengthens us in ways that helps
us keep going. Their love gives us wings.

Affirmation

♥ I am so grateful for all the people in my life
who love me in a way I feel loved

♥ Their ability to love me the right way will continue to grow

♥ My ability to love them the way they need to be loved will increase each day

Inspiration #53

RAINBOW FOCUS

The bridge between regret and giving
something your all is trust.

Trust overrides the fear that leads to regret.

Affirmation

♥ Help me give it my all so I don't live with
regret

♥ I trust that trying is better than not trying at
all

Inspiration #54

Trust makes us feel better. Fear makes us feel worse. I choose trust even if I'm wrong. It just feels better.

Affirmation

♥ Trust helps me feel better

♥ I trust this will work out somehow

Inspiration #55

When we trust, we are doing the right thing. Whenever we do the right thing, it is easier for life to do right by us and show us favor.

Affirmation

♥ Help me trust in the goodness in those that I love

♥ God please help me do the right thing each day

♥ Knowing this formula I can depend on favor becoming a consistent part of my life

Inspiration #56

Please find the support you need. Navigating the tough times is so much better with the right support.

Affirmation

♥ I am opening myself up to receive support and guidance from the right people

Inspiration #57

The right support can help you recognize and work through self-sabotage. We all need this in times of big change or growth. When we are the most uncomfortable, self-sabotage runs wild.

Affirmation

♥ Help me recognize how I self-sabotage

♥ Help me work through it & Pray daily to you

♥ Give me the willpower to resist sabotaging the good things

Inspiration #58

The right support can help us move forward when we feel stuck. Like in those times when it feels like nothing we are doing is working. This is a sign it's time to reach out for help from God, to Pray and have faith in his will for our life

Affirmation

RAINBOW FOCUS

♥ Please give me the courage to reach out for

support from you

Inspiration #59

The right support can lead to feeling loved. When we help each other succeed, love is undeniable. When we know we are loved it's life changing.

Affirmation

♥ I open myself to this deeper sense of feeling loved

Inspiration #60

It's easy to get caught up in the limiting belief that we have to arrive to feel like enough. This is not true. Replace it with, "I am enough just as I am".

Affirmation

♥ I am enough just as I am

♥ I am successful just as I am

♥ I am proud of how far I've come

Inspiration #61

This is for whoever needs to hear this today, "I believe in you."

RAINBOW FOCUS

Affirmation

♥ I believe in me

Inspiration #62

"You can do this! I believe in you."
Sometimes these words are all we need to hear.

Affirmation

♥ I can do this

Inspiration #63

As we move forward in self-belief fear will pop-up. Usually it's the fear of the unknown. Try thinking that the unknown is working in your favor.

Affirmation

♥ The unknown is working in my favor each day

Inspiration #64

When we follow our intuition it can lead us to
the most amazing experiences of our lives.
Trust it. Even when things don't make sense.

Affirmation

♥ I trust with my heart & soul

Inspiration #65

Trust your gut instincts. They will assist in making the right choices.

Affirmation

♥ I trust in my mind to guide me

Inspiration #66

Trust in your abilities. They were given to you
for a reason.

RAINBOW FOCUS

Affirmation

♥ I trust in my abilities to overcome obstacles and to push forward daily to succeed

Inspiration #67

Even when we can't see the good, it is life changing to trust that good is coming from every experience.

Affirmation

♥ I trust that good is in every experience

♥ My time is coming

Inspiration #68

Keep going. Keep running the race you signed up for. Sometimes we have to run in the dark for a while. Before long the dawn will come and you will cross the finish line.

Affirmation

♥ My finish line will come soon for me

♥ My miracle is coming, its on the way to me

Inspiration #69

It's okay to ask for a sign that shows you what you are working toward is on it's way.

Affirmation

♥ Thank you for showing me a sign

Inspiration #70

Once you are certain what you desire is on it's way, it's time to say thank you. "Thank you for bringing me forward

Saying thank you activates trust and releases control over the outcome. It also pulls that thing toward you.

Affirmation

♥ Thank you for bringing me hope

♥ I know what feels right in my soul is meant
for me

Inspiration #71

Keep doing what's right and putting in the
effort. You never know when things can turn
in your favor. Your time will come.

Affirmation

♥ Help me keep doing what's right

♥ My time will come

♥ Help me keep putting in the consistent effort

Inspiration #72

Seek and you will find. Knock and the door
will be opened. Keep seeking and knocking
until you find or the door opens.

Affirmation

♥ If I seek I will find hope

♥ If I keep knocking I will find abundance

RAINBOW FOCUS

Inspiration #73

It's okay to take care of yourself today. As we love ourselves it makes it easier for others to love us. We attract what we do to ourselves.

Affirmation

♥ It's okay to love myself today

♥ It's okay to take care of me

Inspiration #74

RAINBOW FOCUS

Your time will come. I know it may not be
visible, but it is coming.

Affirmation

♥ My time will come, the rainbow will come
for me

Inspiration #75

It may seem like everything is working against you. It's not. Everything is working in your favor. Understanding and clarity will come at the right time.

Affirmation

♥ Understanding and clarity will come

♥ Everything is working in my favor, the clouds are leaving soon and the sunshine and rainbow will come out for me

Inspiration #76

One day you will wake up to a dream come true. I hope that day comes for you soon.

Affirmation

♥ One day my dreams will all come true

♥ My time is coming soon

Inspiration #77

I hope the love you desire comes to you. I also hope you have the courage to let it in.

Affirmation

♥ The love I desire is coming to me

♥ Help me have the courage to let it in the happiness

Inspiration #78

Soon you will wake up happier than you've ever been. When that day comes, cherish it and vow to never take happiness for granted again.

Affirmation

♥ I will never take happiness for granted again

♥ Soon I will be happier than I've ever been before and I will help others to acheive the same success

Inspiration #79

All the good seeds you've sown will produce a harvest. Just keep moving forward and keep planting and you will see your beautiful garden grow for you

Affirmation

♥ My harvest is coming

♥ All the good I put out will come back to me

Inspiration #80

Are you gathering to live or saving for when the sh*t hits the fan? Which one feels lighter? Choose that one.

Affirmation

♥ I am determined to have positive thoughts
and beliefs about money

Inspiration #81

You can have success on your terms if you learn to manage your stress, emotions, and mindset. This is such an empowering truth that will change your life forever. You are more powerful than you think.

Affirmation

♥ I can have success my way

♥ I have the power to manage my stress, emotions and mindset

♥ I am more powerful than I think

Inspiration #82

The world needs to hear your voice. It needs to experience your special gifts deep within. What will it take for you to share awesomeness with the world?

Affirmation

♥ The world needs my special gifts

♥ What will it take for me to share my special gifts with the world?

Inspiration #83

You can overcome the impossible. Persistence and patience mixed with belief are the key in this world

Affirmation

♥ I can overcome the impossible, I can acheive anything that I want for my life

Inspiration #84

Would you like to conquer apathy once and for all? Find a purpose bigger than yourself to live for. This purpose will keep you so motivated every day.

Affirmation

♥ Purpose conquers everything

♥ My purpose can be something small but it can be so great

Inspiration #85

Would you like to see your dreams come true?
Follow your inner guidance. Your soul knows
the way for you

Affirmation

♥ My soul knows the way, with God by my
side

Inspiration #86

Are you ready to live your best life? It's on its way! Just don't give up and don't settle.

Affirmation

♥ My best life is on it's way

♥ My time is coming for me

Inspiration #87

Are you ready for success to be easier? You're in luck! Success becomes easier when we learn to manage our stress and stay calm.

Affirmation

♥ Staying calm equals easier success

♥ Staying calm is a superpower

Inspiration #88

RAINBOW FOCUS

If we live to honor our higher purpose, life will honor us in return. I hold myself to a higher standard because I want the very best from life. Set a higher standard if you want the best from life.

Affirmation

♥ I want the very best from life

♥ I want my life to have true meaning

Inspiration #89

Looking for the good in all things and all people will help you find a better life. This higher standard will raise you to dreams that you never imagined for your life

Affirmation

♥ I want a better life for myself and my family

RAINBOW FOCUS

♥ Help me see the good in the world

♥ Help me see the good in everyone

Inspiration #90

Do you need to hear this today? You can overcome the impossible.

Affirmation

♥ I can overcome the impossible, I can achieve success

Inspiration #91

Allowing the right people to love you will take you higher. Their love will give you wings to overcome anything in life

Affirmation

♥ Love will give me wings to fly high, to acheive my amazing dreams

Inspiration #92

You are almost there. Just keep going. Keep moving forward. You will find a finish line. Once you cross it you can take a vacation.

Affirmation

♥ I am almost there, I can do this, I am worthy of greatness

Inspiration #93

RAINBOW FOCUS

Things will become clear at the right time.
Worrying about it is a waste of time and
energy, life is beautiful

Affirmation

♥ Things will become clear soon

♥ The adversity will turn into joy

Inspiration #94

It's okay to take risks. It's okay to go all in. It's okay to not live with regrets.

Affirmation

♥ I choose to live with no regrets

♥ I am going all in for my dreams

Inspiration #95

Big achievements require a lot of little steps.
Please don't underestimate the importance of
each step.

Affirmation

♥ I will celebrate all the little steps along the way, baby steps are still steps forward and that is fine with me

Inspiration #96

Have the faith, trust and courage to move through your fears. You'll find freedom on the other side of adversity

Affirmation

♥ Faith, trust and courage equal freedom

♥ Thank you for giving me all the courage I need to move through my fears

Inspiration #97

When things become too much, it's okay to slow down. Rest, cry or scream but don't give up. Things will work out for your higher good in my life

Affirmation

♥ Things will work out for me

♥ It's okay to feel like giving up

♥ I trust myself to keep moving forward even if I have to crawl but I will never give up on my amazing dreams

Inspiration #98

RAINBOW FOCUS

Follow the truth of your heart. Honor yourself even in the tough adversity. This will guide you to the best way

Affirmation

♥ I will follow my own heart

♥ I will honor myself even when things get hard

♥ My inner guidance will show me the way to the best outcome

Inspiration #99

Relief is on its way to you. It will show up in unexpected ways and when you least expect it.

Affirmation

♥ Abundance is coming

♥ Joy is coming for me

Inspiration #100

Good things happen to good people. Read
that again. Let it sink in as truth.

Affirmation

♥ I believe good things happen to good people

♥ I release any beliefs that tell me otherwise

♥ Good things are coming into my life

Inspiration #101

Even the toughest experiences can become something good. We have the power to make this a reality. It all begins in our thoughts.

Affirmation

♥ I have the power to make something out of nothing

♥ I am powerful

Inspiration #102

The divine will never give up on you like people will. Take comfort in this and never give up on yourself. I am sorry for those who have given up on you. I believe in you.

Affirmation

♥ God will never give up on me

♥ I will not give up on myself

Inspiration #103

The greatest opportunities come after you
decide to give up yet you keep moving
forward. With new surrender to your goals
comes new levels of opportunity.

Affirmation

♥ It's okay to feel like giving up

♥ It's okay to keep trying even when I don't feel like I can take another step

♥ Somehow this is preparing me for something better

♥ New opportunity are coming my way

I am never giving up on myself or my amazing dreams

Inspiration #104

When your time comes, take a moment to rest in your victory. Relish it. Celebrate how far you have come. Be proud of yourself and what it took you to accomplish your goal.

Affirmation

♥ I am so proud of myself

♥ I finally did it

♥ My abundance and success has come

I wish you beautiful new beginnings and a new you, you are so happy with. A you who feels ready to achieve great things. A you who is full of happiness, joy, and abundance. May this journey brings you love and deep fulfillment. I love all of you. Thank you Thank you Thank you

Thank you, God, for this amazing beautiful life to live my dreams.